LETTER

TO

THE REV. J. A. JAMES,

OF CARR's LANE MEETING HOUSE.

WITH NOTES,

CRITICAL, RELIGIOUS, AND MORAL.

" *Whosoever playeth at* bowls *must expect* rubbers."

OLD SONG.

BY A. BUNN,

MANAGER OF THE THEATRE ROYAL, BIRMINGHAM.

THIRD EDITION.

BIRMINGHAM:

PRINTED FOR THE AUTHOR,

AND MAY BE HAD OF ALL THE BOOKSELLERS.

1824.

ADVERTISEMENT.

I have been principally induced to submit the following pages to public opinion from a perusal of two works, entitled, " The Christian Father's Present to his Children," and " Youth Warned," and from a Sermon delivered some few days since at Carr's Lane Meeting-house, in this town (the nature of which has been conveyed to me), all of which are the productions of the

REV. J. ANGELL JAMES;

and, since its announcement, I have been led to understand, the Reverend Gentleman has expressed his determination to treat me with the greatest contempt—he is quite right—and there we do agree; and if he is desirous of knowing the contempt with which I treat him, he has only to read the following pages.

A. BUNN.

A LETTER, &c.

Birmingham, July 26, 1824.

SIR,

I BEG leave to approach you with all the respect due to your situation, and *particularly due from me*, and acknowledging, as I do, the powerful enemy with whom I am about to contend, I am induced to ask as much indulgence as you can possibly, under the circumstances, grant—for a man so bountifully gifted with Christian *charity*, so well versed in the English language, and on such intimate terms with the Heathen Philosophers,* it must be admitted, is almost too much for the Manager of a Theatre—but having a strong desire to take your opinion on some points, and to doubt it on others, I enter the field accordingly.

The fact is, Mr. JAMES, (as a much greater man† than either you or I, observes), the grand

---

* *James* makes bountiful allusion to those " virtuous Pagans," as he calls them—*Plato, Livy, Xenophon, Cicero, Solon, Cato, Seneca,* and *Tacitus.* One would have supposed a *Christian,* such as JAMES, would not have kept company with a *Pagan.*

† The late *Lord Byron.*

"*primum mobile*" of England now is *cant*; cant political, cant poetical, cant *religious*—cant *moral*—but always cant, multiplied through all the varieties of life, and, as our mutual friend Mr. JOSEPH MILLER would say, when a man *can't* do one thing, he must do another. The principal motive that has induced me to enter upon the *argumentum ad hominem* with you, arises out of a perusal of a late work of your's, entitled "The Christian Father's Present to his Children," and a Sermon, also in print, under the alarming title of "Youth Warned," delivered by you, with sundry others, in Carr's Lane, in this town—and I use not the least hesitation in saying, that a greater mass of grossness, scurrility, and ignorance—of bad* grammar—of bad English, and bad feeling, never came under my perusal before. I have been repeatedly told you are an excellent speaker—be that as it may—I have never heard you—but if you are not a better speaker than you are a writer, I never wish to hear you. The disposition of honest JOHN BULL, however, is such, that he will really put up with most things now-a-days—and it is

---

* As it is foreign to the purpose of this pamphlet to enter into any *grammatical* review of Mr. JAMES's works, and as I entertain no doubt that an opportunity will be afforded me of renewing my argument with that gentleman, I do not think it necessary to institute a critical investigation which may, with more propriety and greater advantage, be adopted hereafter.

not, therefore, to be wondered at, that such continual depredations are daily made upon his credulity, his patience, and his pocket. I think, therefore, a man quite right in probing him to the quick—whether it be in the letting of seats in a Meeting-house, or a Play-house—whether in the preaching a sermon, or in the publishing it, if he can find men weak enough to listen to the one, and purchase the other. There I think him, I say, quite right; but I think him quite wrong to publish any thing he cannot authenticate, or to assert any thing that he cannot prove to be true, and which others can prove to be false—inasmuch as I then consider him a greater fool for printing, than I do the other for purchasing. SHAKSPEARE says, " in which predicament I say thou stand'st," and I am inclined to think SHAKSPEARE in the right.—I will now enter into a review of the different authorities you have advanced in behalf of your arguments, and if you can get yourself out of the difficulty in which I hope to prove you, I shall set you down for a much cleverer fellow, than I have any reason to think you at present. I shall pass over a vast quantity of introductory nonsense about " broad avenues"—" fatal evenings"—" jaws of the devouring lion," and so on, and come to the *jaw* of another animal, equally famed in Scripture—and in as great repute with

Sampson and the Philistines, as it can possibly be at Carr's Lane.

The Stage, from its earliest formation to the present moment, has been considered as the standard of our literary taste, the model of our public oratory, and the pride of our National amusements; and from the support it has received from so many of its members, the great patronage it has always commanded, and the extraordinary genius it has so often elicited, has at once maintained a character high in the scale of nations. It was only at one period, and that in the first Charles's reign, when Puritanism had gained such an alarming ascendancy as eventually to overturn the constitution, that even a *temporary* suspension was given to Theatrical Amusements; and it is by no means a matter of surprise that a blow* which beheaded a king, and deluged the country with blood, should succeed in any suppression of so much less important a nature. It is this same system of fallacy that the Puritans of the present time are daily practising—who, under the sacred cloak of religion, are amassing wealth, personal aggrandizement, and general power; and in most cases committing those alarming excesses,

* The reader is requested to understand that I do not refer to a *political* question—whether it was right or whether it was wrong—of which I *know* just as much as I *care.* I merely quote the circumstance as a theatrical *date.*

compared to which the follies and extrava-
gancies of the stage are eminent virtues. Your
" pungent" friend PRYNNE, whose " Catalogue
of Authorities" you allude to on every occasion, and who is also cited by STYLES, of
Brighton, was one of those precious impostors,
and a reference to Rushworth's State Trials
will prove him to be one of the greatest vaga-
bonds that ever escaped the gallows.* With
this solitary exception, the stage has maintained an undisputed rank among the most eminent
and instructive schools in which genius and
learning have ever appeared, or been nourished.
Having thus, therefore, disposed of your
friend PRYNNE and his pungency, let us pro-
ceed to examine " the more virtuous Pagans"
who, you assert, condemned the amusements
of the Theatre, as injurious to morals and the
interests of nations. In looking over the list
of names you have introduced, and which, by

---

* This said William Prynne, whose productions are styled by
James " admirable," for the publication of a book called *Histrio-
Mastyx*, decrying stage-plays, music, dancing, hunting, public festi-
vals, christmas keeping, &c. for blaming the hierarchy, and the
ceremonies in religious worship, and designating our Saviour a
Puritan, was condemned to stand in the pillory in two places—
Westminster and Cheapside—to lose both his ears—one in each
place—to pay £5000 to the King, and to be imprisoned during life.
See Rushworth's State Trials, vol. 2. pp. 220, 221, &c.—A precious
rascal! And, between ourselves, Mr. James, there are *one* or two puritans I could name, to whom the lopping off an ear or two, like
your friend Prynne, would be of infinite service.

the way, with nearly the whole of your book, you have borrowed, word for word, from *Doctor* STYLES, (as you call him, but whose best claim to the title of DOCTOR is, his being a *quack*),* I find, Sir, you have made a miserable blunder—first of all, by omitting such names as *Socrates* and *Aristotle* among the venerable men of antiquity, and including *Cicero, Solon,* and *Seneca,* as denouncers of Theatrical Amusements. The difference between what you have asserted, and the—truth, is, that in the first place, *Socrates,* the most celebrated of philosophers, and one of the wisest men that ever lived, not only gave a general countenance to the Drama, but assisted his pupil, *Euripides,* in the composition of some of that great poet's most established tragedies ; and *Aristotle,* whom *Plato* calls the Philosopher of Truth, laid down a model for the formation and arrangement of the Greek Stage. In the next place, *Cicero,* who was the pupil of *Roscius,* the famous Roman Comedian, has handed down to us some important principles for the organization of a great actor,† and has acknowledged that he derived consider-

---

* What will be said, when it is understood that the said *Styles,* after deprecating in the provinces (where he is getting his livelihood) all Theatrical Amusements, *has been seen* in the lobbies of Drury Lane and Covent Garden, and at Vauxhall Gardens.—" Their best conscience is—not to leave *undone*—but keep *unknown.*" *Othello.*

† Cic. de Orat. Lib. 1.

able force and polish from the precepts and *examples* of his friend *Roscius**—in his defence of the poet, *Archias*, has made high and honourable mention of him, and, on an accusation being preferred against him, *Cicero* undertook his defence, and in one of his most eloquent orations cleared him of the charge. *Cicero's* opinion may be summed up by quoting a passage when he observes, that " the excellencies of *Roscius* became at length proverbial, and the greatest praise that could be given to men of genius in any particular profession, was, that each was a *Roscius* in his art."†
Again, *Solon* the wise, although he expressed such high indignation at the representation of some parts of the tragedies of *Thespis*, is known to have frequented plays in his decline of life;—the death of *Draco*,‡ the lawgiver, and one of the seven wise men of Greece, will sufficiently testify *his* sanction of the Stage;—and *Plutarch* considered the public spectacles of his country as useful to polish its manners, and instil in her children the principles of virtue. *Seneca*, also, the stern moralist and philosopher (mark, reader! another

---

* " Think of that, Master Brooke"—Roscius the *actor*, the *friend* of CICERO!

† Jamdiu consecutus est ut in quo quisquis artifex excelleret is in suo genere *Roscius* diceretur. Cic. de Orat. lib. I.

‡ Plut. in Sol.

of Mr. JAMES's " pagan" friends), according to *Quintilian*, composed the tragedy of *Medea*, and, on the authority of others, the *Troas* and *Hyppolitus* were also written by him ;—but it is placed so far beyond doubt how essential the Athenians considered dramatic representations to the enlargement of their understandings, and the support of their liberties, that an hundred thousand pounds are said to have been expended on one single tragedy of *Sophocles*. Having merely quoted the above *authorities* as flat contradictions to that part of your assertions to which they refer, I think it as well to make a reference to the estimation of the Stage among the Ancients. generally, by remarking, that, at the most flourishing period of both Greece and Rome, the Drama received a sanction from the legislature and populace beyond every other pursuit of those countries —and the very brightest names of antiquity, the very wisest and best of men, have been her firmest advocates and first supporters.

It is impossible for any state to have been more jealous of its liberties than Athens, or more sensible that corruption and debauchery were fatal to its prerogatives ; and no nation exercised such severity against the slightest violation of order. Yet knowing that the freedom of the Theatre, next to the freedom of the Senate, was the surest promotion of general liberty, and the best bulwark against the undermining of any sect or party that might attempt to sap its foundation, they evinced an universal encouragement of the Stage—not for the sake of exhibiting pompous spectacles for the gratification of idleness, and assemblage of folly, but for the encouragement of the most rational, instructive, and pleasing compositions that human talent had then arrived at, and most worthy the entertainment of a warlike and wise nation.

As the arts and sciences increased at Rome, when, with the advance of her fortunes, the genius of her sons spread over the world, and when learning consequently flourished, the first of her Statesmen, Warriors, and Poets, gave the sanction of their abilities, the eloquence of their tongues and pens, and the best energies of their feelings, in support of the Drama. *Lælius*, surnamed the wise, and *Scipio Africanus*, one of the greatest of her warriors, are recorded as the associates and friends of *Terence*, and supposed, on the best authorities, to have assisted him in the compositions of his Comedies. The learned *Varro**

* Postquam morte captus est Plautus
    Comædia luget, scena est deserta ;
    Deinde risus, ludus, jocusque, & numeri
    Innumeri simul omnes collacrymârunt.
There's a touch of Latin for you, Mr. JAMES! and *Varro*, depend upon it, was no fool !

has passed the highest possible eulogium on the Comedies of *Plautus,* which still kept possession of the Stage in the reign of *Diocletian,* a period of more than 500 years from their composition, despite of every change of manner, or influence of opinion, and amid all the revolutions of government. The mighty *Cæsar,* who, in addition to the splendor of his warlike genius, was an eminent poet and writer, mentions *Terence* and *Menander* with great respect—and *Augustus Cæsar,* whom tradition distinguishes for his extraordinary patronage of learning, for his great benevolence, and also for his own literary acquirements—and whose reign will be recorded while the world exists, as being the one in which the Saviour of that world was born, wrote the Tragedy of *Ajax* and other Plays. *Brutus,* one of the purest models of heathen morality and virtue, thought it essential to travel from Rome to Naples, for the purpose of seeing a Company of Comedians, at a time when the State was violently agitated by the murder of *Cæsar*—and, on witnessing their exertions, despatched them to Rome, with letters of recommendation to *Cicero,* under the impression that nothing could so effectually tranquillize the public mind as the preceptive lessons of the Drama.

Let us now, Mr. JAMES, descend from Paganism to Christianity, and take a slight review of the stage in its later and present situation; and again referring to your authorities, I find you *as well informed* on *this* point, as upon the other. When you quote the *motion* of the American Congress, soon after its declaration of independence, you must surely have been *moved* yourself, or you would have been aware, that in no country has the Drama received more general sanction than in America, and up to the present moment it is a principal speculation with our transatlantic friends; and among her wisest and ablest men, is in the highest state of cultivation. In our own country, after the restoration of the stage to its original privileges, with the accession of Charles the Second, the Drama rose to the highest pitch of public favour, and has continued, as being one of the most comprehensive and enlightened, so one of the most favoured amongst all the professions of science and acquirement. The name of one individual is a distinction to it that no other art can boast of— a name that, so long as one stone of the world is left upon another, and one man left to contemplate the ruins, can never be obliterated from his memory—*Shakspeare!*"* Sum up " the

---

* JAMES must not consider this personal, because I think that *Shakspeare's* works will survive *even* the " pious orgies" that emanate from Carr's-lane Meeting-house.

deliberate acts of fifty-four ancient and modern, general, national, provincial councils and synods, both of the Western and Eastern Churches; the condemnatory sentence of seventy-one ancient and one hundred and fifty modern Popish and Protestant authors—the hostile endeavours of philosophers, and even poets—the legislative enactments of a great number of Pagan and Christian states, nations, magistrates, emperors, and princes," and throw the works of JAMES, *Styles*, and *Billy Prynne*, into the bargain, and the whole of them will not contain a hundredth part of the genius to be found in *any one* play of *Shakspeare*, and not more religious conviction than is manifested in *most* of them.*

That name is of itself sufficient testimony of the talent with which the Stage is supported—but in addition to that, we have to record some of the most splendid† that have ever adorned the pages of English history. Some of our

---

* .... Alas, alas!
Why all the souls that were, were forfeit once;
And HE that might the 'vantage best have took,
Found out the remedy: How would you be
If HE, which is the top of judgment, should
But judge YOU *as you* ARE?
      Shakspeare's Measure for Measure.

This one passage has more sense, sound religion, and above all, TRUTH, in it, than all the *canting* pretensions of the above fellows put together.

† Without unnecessarily swelling the list, I may mention the names (though not Divines) of *Beaumont, Fletcher, Johnson, Massinger, Shirley, Ford, Webster, Marlow, Lily, Dryden, Otway,*

most eminent divines and most pious characters are to be found in the list. The mighty
Milton, author of *Paradise Lost*, composed the
popular Masque of *Comus*, originally peformed
by some of the Nobility at Ludlow Castle,
which *Dr. Johnson* styles the greatest of that
author's early performances ; he likewise
wrote *Sampson Agonistes*, the foundation of
which story is to be found in the bible,*—and
the Masque of *Arcades*. The pious *Addison*
is the author of the tragedy of *Cato*, the opera
of *Rosamond*, and the comedy of the *Drummer*.
Dr. Johnson, our great moralist, was the bosom friend of *Garrick*, our great actor, continually frequented theatres, and wrote the tragedy of *Irene*. *Dr. Young*, the distinguished
author of the *Night Thoughts*, wrote the tragedies of the *Revenge, Busiris*, and the *Brothers* †
Thomson, the author of the *Seasons*, a pious,
good man, and whose *Hymn* is worth more
than all the productions of the Puritans
en masse, is the author of five *tragedies* and a

Rowe, Southern, Congreve, Farquhar, Cibber, and the great *Pope*,
who, though not a play-wright himself, thus mentions their object :
    " To melt the soul by tender strokes of art,
    " To raise the genius, and to mend the heart."
Prologue to Cato.
With *Murphy, Goldsmith, Cumberland, Colman, Sheridan,* and a whole
host of others.

  * Judges, chap. xiii.

  † The profits, arising from three performances of this play were
given by the Author to promote the Propagation of the Gospel in
Foreign Parts.

masque.*   *Lillo*, a Protestant Dissenter, amongst a variety of works, has left behind him the tragedy of *George Barnwell*;† probably more generally represented than any Drama in possession of the stage, and which, from its beautiful but simple language, its domestic

---

* *Sophonisba, Agamemnon, Edward and Eleonora, Alfred, Tancred and Sigismunda,* and *Coriolanus.*

† One of the most extraordinary instances on record, is an incident that arose out of a representation of this play. A young clerk, whose follies had placed him precisely in the situation of *George Barnwell*—who, by the intrigues of a wanton, had defrauded his Master of £200, was taken alarmingly ill, and in an interview with his Physician, *Dr. Barrowby*, confessed the whole of the circumstances, from an impression created on his mind by seeing *Mr. Ross* and *Mrs. Pritchard* in the principal characters. The Doctor communicated the case to the youth's father, who paid the money instantly—the son recovered—and became an eminent merchant and a sound Christian—and in a letter from *Ross* to a friend, dated 20th of August, 1787, are these words:

   " Though I never knew his name, or saw him to my knowledge,
" I had for nine or ten years, at my benefit, a note sealed up with
" ten guineas, and these words, ' *A tribute of gratitude from one who*
" ' *was highly obliged, and saved from ruin, by seeing* Mr. Ross's *per-*
" ' *formance of* George Barnwell.' "

What say you to this, Master JAMES? It is a question in my mind whether " Youth Warned" will ever have this effect. The odds are decidedly on *Barnwell !*

   This is not the only instance where

        .... Guilty creatures, sitting at a play,
        Have by the very cunning of the scene
        Been struck so to the soul, that presently
        They have proclaimed their malefactions.

                               Hamlet.

interest and forcible **example**, will **never lose** its present estimation.

*Mason,** a man equally valued by the world for his virtues and writings, is the author of *Elfrida, Caractacus*, and other dramatic works. The *Rev. Dr. Brown* is author of the tragedies of *Barbarossa* and *Athelstan*. The *Rev. John Home*, with five other tragedies, is author of one of the most popular ones in our language, viz. *Douglas*—and although that canting dunce Styles, says, " with regard to its aspect on Christianity† it is exceedingly dangerous," possesses some of the purest language, and best precept the hand need pen, or the ear listen to —but it little matters what *styles* the readers of such men as these adopt—for I find at page 95 of the *Doctor's* lucubrations, that he says " The good man of the Theatre, who receives the plaudits of a Christian audience, is not a Christian; his principles are taught in a seminary *where Christ has no authority*." Any one who *styles* this any thing but downright PROFANENESS and FALSEHOOD is worse than

---

* *Mr. Mason* was Rector of Aston in Yorkshire, Canon Residentiary and Precentor of York Cathedral, and Prebendary of Driffield. *This* looks well, Mr. James!

† What *Styles* means by an " aspect *on* Christianity," I have not the remotest idea.

the *Doctor* himself. *Tate* and *Brady*,* the well known versifiers of DAVID's Psalms, both wrote for the Stage—*Tate*, the tragedies of *Brutus of Alba*, and *The Loyal General*, and eight or nine other plays, and *Brady*, the tragedy of the *Rape*.

The *Rev. Dr. Franklin*, chaplain to his late Majesty, is the author of the *Earl of Warwick*, and many other original and translated pieces. The *Rev. Dr. Ridley*, considered a most worthy divine, and as such recorded in a beautiful Latin epitaph by *Dr. Lowth*, Bishop of London, not only composed the tragedies of *Jugurtha* and the *Faithless Redress*, but is said to have represented with considerable effect, the characters of *Marc Antony, Jaffier, Horatio*, and *Moneses*, at Midhurst, in Sussex, where he used to perform in a Private Theatre with the *Rev. Dr. Thomas Fletcher*, (afterwards Bishop of Kildare) *Dr. Eyre*, and others, who aided him in the composition of the last-named tragedy.

But if it were necessary to enter into any more copious account of the numerous Divines who have contributed the splendor of their talents equally to the advancement of the Drama as to the propagation of the Gospel, I might mention the names of *Stockdale, Strode,*

---

* *Dr. Hugh Brady* was a Clergyman, Rector of Clapham, and Chaplain to William and Mary, and Queen Anne.

Langhorne, Townley, Trapp, Hoadley, Banister, cum multis aliis; and, in the present day, some very excellent writers for the stage are Members of the Church of England. The *Rev. Mr. Milman* is author of one of our finest tragedies,* and some dramatic poems. The *Rev. Charles Maturin* is also a successful dramatist ; and *Croly* has just lashed, in a popular comedy, some of the reigning follies of the moment. To these names we may add the *Rev. James Plumtree,* who has printed four discourses (previously preached at Great St. Mary's Church, Cambridge), and also written the comedy of *The Coventry Act* and the tragedy of *Osway.* But, as we go on, we shall find, Mr. JAMES, that *Mrs. Hannah More,* whom you and *Styles* are continually quoting as authorities in advancement of your opinions, is the authoress of several tragedies† and sacred dramas ; and another Lady,‡ whose opinions you seem to deal in pretty freely, is one of our very first dramatic writers now living, and yet one of the best christians, I believe, that ever did live, though she does not profess puritanical principles.

---

* *Fazio, The Fall of Jerusalem, Martyr of Antioch,* and *Belshazzar's Feast,* are *Mr. Millman's* dramatic works.

† One of them, *Percy,* was lately revived at Covent Garden Theatre, for the performance of *Elwina* by the late *Miss O'Neil.*

‡ *Miss Joanna Baillie.*

With all these proofs, therefore, before you, I must either write you down for any thing but a scholar, or nothing but a bigot—which I know not—nor does it matter—for admitting you to be the former, learning so applied can only mislead—and if the latter, prejudice so directed can only injure.

From this part of our controversy, I shall briefly touch on your idea of the tendency of the Drama, and the general character of its representatives—and in opposition to that part of your argument, where you assert that the bad passions which christianity is intended to extirpate from the human bosom, are inculcated by the most popular Tragedies (which opinion is worth about as much as any other you have given) I shall quote *Aristotle* in his definition of Tragedy, who thus expresses himself: " Tragedy is the imitation of an ac- " tion, which, by means of *terror* and *com-* " *passion*, refines and purifies in us all sorts " of passion ;" and the pious Emperor *Marcus Aurelius*,* who has passed the same kind

---

☞ Perhaps it may not be irrelevant here to observe, that the earliest formation of the Drama is founded on the Holy Bible—and that its *preachers* were the principal *performers*—but they were found to be such horribly *bad* ACTORS, that it soon got into " better hands," and has consequently arrived at its present state of perfection. But as I shall probably *have occasion* to address JAMES again, I will delay any accounts of the miracle plays and mysteries for " the hereafter."

* Chap. vi. 9th book of his Reflections.

of judgment on it when he says, " Tragedies
" were first introduced to put men in mind
" of those accidents which happen in their
" lives—to inform them, they must necessarily
" come, and teach them that these things they
" see with so much delight on the Stage should
" not appear insupportable in the grand
" theatre of the world." I suppose it is hardly
necessary to tell you, that I think both *Aristotle* and *Aurelius* better judges than you,
Mr. JAMES---and, to say the *least* of them, as good
men. There can be no doubt that the aim of
tragedy is not only to purify the passions, but
to elevate the understanding—to behold virtue
made beautiful, and vice rendered odious—and
although this branch of the art may hold the
more elevated position amongst its productions,
yet, whether viewed in its support of tragedy or
comedy, this high and interesting profession has
but one purpose, " whose end, both at the first,
" and now, was, and is, to hold as 'twere the
" mirror up to nature : to show virtue her own
" feature, scorn her own image, and the very
" age and body of the time his form and pres-
" sure."* I could adduce (were it necessary
so to do, beyond what I have already advanced)
numerous instances of the application of this
splendid passage to the general formation of
the Drama—but having already alluded to

* Hamlet.

one strong case in the instance of *George Barnwell*, the only additional elucidation necessary, in the extent of our *comedies*, is the general advantage and powerful support brought forward, in that of the *Hypocrite**— where a forcible example is illustrated of the attempt of fanaticism to undermine the principle, property, and virtue of society, for its own individual advantage, and under the specious garb of religion, to render crime a kind of pastime. This exemplification fully bears out the opinions given by *Cicero* of comedy, where he remarks that " it is the *imitation of life*,† the mirror of manners, and the representation of truth—*Imitatio vitæ, speculum consuetudinis, imago veritatis.* As my limits will not admit of a more extended view of the properties or advantages of dramatic representations, it will be

---

* The selection of this comedy for his Majesty's patronage, during the last season at Drury Lane, appears to me a step of the first policy and prudence (an impression particularly discernible in its enjoyment by the King himself)—for it must have been apparent to the Legislators of the Crown, and the Royal Advisers, that the effect of its representation would tend, *as it has*, to annihilate a considerable portion of that puritanical influence which, under a profane pretence of paying worship to the CREATOR, is daily deceiving and robbing HIS *creatures*.

I think, Mr. JAMES, it would not puzzle either *you* or me much, to find a *Doctor Cantwell* among *some* of our acquaintance !

† And what better *imitation* of *life* can there be than the *Cantwell*, *Mawworm*, and *Old Lady Lambert* of the *Hypocrite.*

sufficient to observe, that at the present moment the Stage has to boast of the highest and most extensive patronage of the land—the personal sanction of our Gracious Monarch, of his principal Divines, Statesmen, Chieftains, and Poets—and did I not know, by the doctrines laid down by yourself and your disciples, the narrowness of your views, and the ignorance of your pretensions, I should cite that presumption which could decry a profession *so* patronized, as the result of an incoherent intellect—but as it is, I consider it the political aim of party endeavouring to divert the public mind from a source of enjoyment, the contributions to which necessarily prevent their giving *as much support* to religious influences and persuasions, as the cupidity of its self-created Ministers aim at the possession of.

It has now become necessary to treat your argument in a religious view—but as I am perfectly aware of my own inability in this respect, and am of opinion the less discussion entertained on *such* a point the better, I shall endeavour to be as brief as possible. You suppose " that the most passionate admirers of the Stage will not try it in a court of christianity," and observe, that " any one who asserts it is in accordance with its doctrines, precepts, examples, spirit, or design, really insults

common sense." You suppose wrong, for *I* as
sert it—and will endeavour to prove it. I will
simply apply to any one who has made it his study,
and is consequently well versed in the grand
compendium of christianity—and ask, if the life,
words, and actions of *Man's* REDEEMER do
not bear full testimony to what I avow, by the
sanction therein given to proper recreation,
under whatever form it appear. At the æra of
our SAVIOUR'S existence, and during the so-
journ of himself and his Apostles in that city,
there was a Theatre in Jerusalem—as also in
many other places through which they travelled;
and yet in all their works, when they went
forth by divine command to " convert all nations," and extirpate vice and immorality from
the land, no one instance can be found con-
demning the amusements of the Stage, though
crime and folly of the most minute description
is elsewhere severely reproved by them. This
is sufficient testimony that the drama never in-
curred the censure of the Gospel—but I am
prepared to shew that in several instances it
has been sanctioned by it. The words used by
yourself in speaking of a theatre, viz. " Vice
in every form *lives and moves, and has its being
there,*" are taken by you from *St. Paul,* Acts
xvii. 28,* which, by *his own confession,* St.

* Acts xvii. 28—" For in him we live and move, and have our
being, *as certain also of* YOUR OWN POETS *have said,* for we are
also HIS offspring."

Paul quotes from one of the Greek dramatists Another instance occurs in that celebrated line " Evil communications corrupt good manners,"* which is quoted by *St. Paul* from the tragedy of *Iphigenia*, by *Euripides*, who flourished above 400 years before Christ—and in his Epistle to Titus, chap. 1, ver. 12, 13, speaking of the people of Crete, he says, " One of themselves, even a *Prophet* of their own, said, the Cretans are always liars, evil beasts, slow bellies, This *witness is true*, &c." which passage is to be found in Epimenides,† who lived 290 years before Christ, word for word. The reader will here perceive that the Apostle not only quotes a heathen poet, but designates him with the title of *Prophet*—which is the most convincing argument I can possibly adduce, that had the tendency of the stage been such as it is classed by you, the most learned of all the Apostles, in delivering the divine oracles of God, would never have incorporated sayings that had probably been spoken a hundred times on the public stage in the Gospel of Truth, notwithstanding all their morality or innocence of expression.‡

* 1 Corinthians, chap. xv. v. 33.

† " Κρῆτες ἀεί Ψευϛαί, κακα θηρία, γαϛερες ἀργαί."

Epimenides.

‡ " As the Spirit of God spoke by the inspired Apostles, we may " venture to boast it gives some reputation to the *Poet*, and sure a " little vindication of the increase of the *profession*, that the Holy

But the very object of the stage is the advancement of religion—whether with reference to that part which embodies *things to be believed*, viz.—the Being of a God—Providence—immortality of the soul—future rewards and punishments—or to that part which embodies *things to be done,* including our duty to God—our duty to our neighbour—and our duty to ourselves. In furtherance of all these points, I boldly assert it is the object of the Drama to assist; since the moral of all its works, is, the reward of goodness, punishment of crime, and general recommendation of the christian virtues.— If the thing were not too apparent, I could cite the principal Tragedies and Comedies in our language—but that would be superfluous; and having, therefore, placed this general conviction before your eyes, I can only, when I behold your utter ignorance of Gospel as applied to your argument, trace your inveteracy against the stage to the exposition it gives of hypocrisy, and those of its concomitant feelings, which naturally makes men averse to fanaticism and the affected austerity of bigots, and which is the reason why Jesuits on the one hand, and fanatics on the other, have ever maintained the same animosity—and it is equally remarkable, as *Den-*

" Ghost himself has spoken in the words of a *Menander* and an
" *Epimenides.*"—DENNIS.

nis observes, that the Church and the Hierarchy since the Reformation have flourished with the Stage—were deposed with it, and restored with it.—Since I have applied *some* quotations from the Gospel to *my* profession, I cannot do better than also apply it to the profession of *others*, and, having so done, we will conclude *this* part of our argument :—

Ver. 13.—Woe unto you, Scribes and Pharisees, *hypocrites!* for *ye shut up the Kingdom of Heaven against men.*

Ver. 14.—Woe unto you, Scribes and Pharisees, *hypocrites!* for *ye devour* widows' *houses*, and for a pretence make *long prayer;* therefore ye shall receive the greater damnation.

Ver. 15.—Woe unto ye, Scribes and Pharisees, *hypocrites!* for ye compass sea and land to make one proselyte; and when he is made, ye make him twofold more the child of hell than yourselves.

Ver. 16.—Woe unto you, ye blind guides, which say, whosoever shall swear by the temple, it is nothing; but whosoever shall swear by the *gold* of the temple, he is a debtor,

St. Matthew, *chap.* 23.

And now let me advert to the arrogant manner in which you have thought proper to speak of those who are the representatives of our national Drama. As there is no medium through which men's actions can be so minutely viewed, or dissected as the Stage, it follows that the nature of them must be better known; and yet, labouring under all this disadvantage, I will undertake to say, that, as a profession, it is tainted with less real crime and immoral conduct than many others, and decidedly less than is to be found among many of the advocates, *as they are called,* of religion. Among the numerous religious denominations* are to be found characters of the very worst description. We almost daily hear, with a shudder, of some alarming inroad made on the morals of society, and the *common decencies* of life—of thefts, forgeries, adulteries, and seductions—of every abuse of those precepts it is the function of their high office to instil—of administration to the dying sinner, for the sole purpose of possessing his wealth—and of undermining, generally, the noblest impulses of the heart. I deprecate crime, folly, or excess, in all its influences on man's conduct, as much as any man can; but I consider the worst deed committed under the pangs of want, or any misdirection of the mind, is virtually to be *palliated,* compared with those which are done under the appearance of religion, thereby offering a tenfold insult to the DEITY, by the addition of hypocrisy to the commitment of sin, and using the dictates of a HEAVENLY POWER for the furtherance of EARTHLY GUILT. Among the other opinions you so liberally give of the

---

* *Smith,* the Missionary, is one instance—and the late convictions of *Emma George,* for the murder of her brother, and *Samuel Broadbent,* a married man, *thirty-eight* years of age, for an assault on a child *ten* years of age, furnishes two others.

" players," I perceive you say " Players have no *leisure* to learn to die;*" and in another passage talk of their " *indolent* line of life—contrarieties that I confess I do not understand ; but how that profession is to be stigmatised as *idle* that calls into operation every faculty of the mind and body—a profession that demands a knowledge of history, philosophy, divinity—of language—of philology—indeed of general science—(for there is no art so rigid in its exactions, or so exorbitant in its requisitions) how this can be designated an *idle* course of life, I know not; and they who do not make these principles the rudiments and foundation of their dramatic education, may vainly aspire to any perfection in their undertaking. That hundreds do not, I am ready to admit ; and that the Stage possesses as many hundreds of unworthy members is equally apparent; but it is not so much to be wondered at, when I consider that many men, after going through all the vagabondry of life, enter into a profession for which they are not half so well fitted as for the gibbet, and where a supply of impudence affects, for their purposes, what a deficiency of

---

* How this may be with some *Preachers* I know not—but that they find time to *learn to* LIVE is pretty evident—and a capital job they make of it too !

understanding never could. It is this inroad continually made on the Stage, that has subjected its ornamental members to such unmerited obloquy ; but as long as the Drama can boast of the great names whose moral character and splendid abilities have adorned, and still do, her pages and her boards, she may lift her head as high as any of her sister arts. Her children labour under disadvantages (as is evident from the above remark) that no other advocates do—for men of the lowest origin and meanest intellect have, by assurance and ambition, jumped into a pulpit, and amassed more money in a few years, than a whole life devoted to any other pursuit they might have embarked in could ever have realized them. You also remark, " as to the feelings of *modern times*, is there a family in Britain of the least moral worth, even among the middling class of tradesmen, which would not feel itself disgraced if any of its members were to embrace this profession ?" Matchless impudence and falsehood ! You are not ignorant that three of England's Coronets at this hour are worn by Actresses; and that the eminent virtues and abilities which distinguished *Miss Farren, Miss Brunton,* and *Miss Bolton,* ON the stage, now adorn the *Countesses of Derby* and *Craven* and *Lady Thurlow* OFF it—aye, and with a sevenfold lustre compared with many who are born to this hereditary chaplet. You are not ignorant that the stage at this present moment has to boast of many performers of both sexes, whose genius would adorn any profession, and whose character would add splendour to any society—and as highly remarkable for purity of heart and christian principle, as any individuals on the earth—and far more so than thousands who, for the purpose of blinding the world, adopt an " *outward sign*" that has no " *inward spiritual grace.*"

And here I may venture, I hope, without the charge of vanity on my own part, or disrespect to others, to allude to the dearest branch of my family—and I assert, without a fear of exciting either the envy or ill will of a friend or enemy, that in all the congregations of the country, or in any of its relative associations, is not to be found a more virtuous character, or better christian, than MY OWN WIFE, who, stepping out of the walks of private life, embraced a profession to which the public has been pleased to consider her an ornament; and so far from deeming the connection a *disgrace* (as you dare to term it) she has the greatest pride in regarding it a high and distinguished honour. I am aware that this particular case is a very delicate one for me to touch upon; but I should consider that man unworthy a situation in society who could read such an unmanly and gross calumny cast on the profession to which any member of his family belonged, (and which of course must equally apply to them, as to others,) and not feel all the warmest and strongest impulses of the human heart rise up to repel the infamous assertion.

I find you also say that " the Theatre is one of the broadest avenues which lead to destruction, and all the evils that can waste man's *property*, corrupt his morals, blast his reputation, impair his health, embitter his life, and *destroy his soul*, lurk in its purlieus." Now I will tell you how far we differ on this point—and, without going into any further analysis of this passage, I will content myself by quoting two very eminent writers, in direct contradiction to your assertion, and save myself the trouble of going into any further argument, although it is evident that the universal sanction of mankind, and the custom of ages, is sufficient refutation of your contemptible, arrogant, and incorrect statement.

" If the Theatre," says *La Motte* in his ingenious *Essay on Poetry and Painting*, " were to be shut up, the Stage wholly silenced and suppressed, I believe the world, bad as it is now, would be then ten times more wicked and debauched"—" which," says *Mr. Wilkes* in his admirable *View of the Stage,* " was once the case at Milan : when *Charles Barromeus* took possession of the Archbishopric, he, out of abundance of zeal and severity, shut up the play-house, and expelled the players, strollers, and minstrels, as debauchers and corrupters of mankind. He soon had reason to alter his opinion, for he found that the people run into all manner of excesses ; and that wanting something to amuse and divert them, they committed the most horrid crimes by way of pastime. It was on this account he repented of his edict, recalled the banished players, and granted them a free use and liberty of the stage."— So much for Mr. JAMES and his *morals.*

I will now bring the present address to a close, and reserve my further remarks for any future opportunity that may present itself. The result of my disquisition and of my general arguments is briefly summed up, and supposing you may be anxious to know what it is, I use no hesitation in giving my opinion that you are an *Angel,* JAMES, but I am equally of opinion, you are a *fallen* one.

A. BUNN.

POSTSCRIPT.

THE Reader *is requested to understand, that the purport of the preceding pages is directed rather against the unwarrantable attack made by an individual, than against the community over whom that individual presides; and I can confidently avow, that if Mr.* JAMES *had not gone so far out of the path of his duty as to overstep the bounds of* Christian Feeling, Charity, *and* Truth, *by inveighing in terms of gross scurrility against a profession, the principles of which, though not in unison with his own, are sanctioned by millions of his fellow creatures, I should never have thought of addressing him. I am sensible that some of the worthiest men in Birmingham are followers of Mr. James's doctrines, and so they might continue " to the end o' time" before I should presume to interfere with their opinions; but as I am aware that there may be some of the*

most unworthy also attend him, I can only say,
with reference to what I have written, that
" whomsoever the cap fitteth, by him let the cap
" be worn."

A. B.

FINIS.

T. DEWSON, PRINTER.